GARY FRAZIER

IT COULD HAPPEN TOMORROW

UNDERSTANDING FUTURE EVENTS THAT WILL SHAKE THE WORLD

SAMPSON RESOURCES
4887 Alpha Rd, Ste 220
Dallas, Texas 75244
800-371-5248 Fax 972-387-0150
www.sampsonresources.com   info@sampsonresources.com

HOW TO USE THE PARTICIPANT BOOK

The *It Could Happen Tomorrow* participant book is designed to accompany the 8-session video study by Gary Frazier. This book includes a narrative section at the beginning of each lesson that contains the content of Dr. Frazier's video lesson, as well as a discussion and application section, and prayer. If at all possible, every participant should have a book to use in the study and to keep as a valuable resource for years to come. (All Scripture – King James Version)

TABLE OF CONTENTS

GLOSSARY

Antichrist, The – The false Messiah, energized by Satan, who will arise in opposition to God, Christianity and Israel just prior to Christ's Coming (2 Thess. 2.3-10).

Apocalypse – Literally, an unveiling, that is, a revealing of a person or thing in its true character. Synonymous with revelation, and an alternate title for the book of Revelation. Because of its association with the "end of the world," apocalypse is sometimes used to denote a radical destruction or purge.

Apocalyptic – Pertaining to the end of the world, or to some awesome destruction.

Apostasy – A spiritual falling away, i.e., a rebellion, as described in 2 Thessalonians 2.3.

Armageddon – Literally, *the mountain of Megiddo.* The name given to the valley below the ancient city (now a ruin) of Megiddo in northern Israel. Also the name given to the final eschatological battle for Jerusalem, since the military staging for the battle will occur at the valley of Megiddo. It represents the end of the militant enemies of Messiah who are consumed by His coming.

End Time, The – The epoch in which some of God's people will be refined by tribulation (Dan. 11.33-35), as a rebel king affronts Messiah (Dan. 8.17-25), and invades Israel (Dan. 11.40-45). It is the apocalyptic time leading up to the resurrection and judgment (Dan. 12.1-2).

Eschatology – The study of last things, that is, the final events of redemption described in Bible prophecy. Derived from the Greek word meaning *last.*

Millennial Kingdom, Millennial Reign – The 1,000-year earthly kingdom set up by Christ at his second coming.

Millennium – The thousand-year period during which Christ will reign on earth after his second coming, and during which Satan will be bound.

Postmillennialism – Belief in the restoration of society, primarily through the influence of the church, before the return of Christ. It is the return of Christ that is post, i.e., after, the millennium. This view tends to equate the "millennium" with "the church age."

Post-tribulationist – One who believes that Christ will rapture Christians *after* the Great Tribulation.

Premillennialism – Belief in a literal coming of Christ before the 1,000 -year reign of world peace.

Pre-tribulationist – One who believes that Christ will rapture Christians *before* the beginning of the Great Tribulation.

Rapture – Literally, a catching up, based on the Latin word used in the Vulgate version of 1 Thessalonians 4.17. It refers to the catching up to the clouds of Christians who are alive at the coming of Christ, immediately preceded by the resurrection of Christians who have already died.

Second Coming, The – Also "Second Advent" or "Glorious Appearing." The return of Christ in glory, as differentiated from his first coming in humiliation. Christ will return in bodily form to destroy his enemies and glorify his elect. (See Acts 1.11.)

Lesson 1

Introduction & Overview

I am so glad that you have decided to participate in this study of biblical prophecy – *It Could Happen Tomorrow: Future Events That Will Shake the World*. For generations, many dedicated students of the Bible, including some Christian leaders, have resisted teaching and preaching on biblical prophecy; so I want to congratulate you on making this choice. I pray that you will be blessed by every moment you spend in these lessons studying God's Word.

This first lesson is critical because it serves as an introduction to the entire study and an overview of what we will examine in all eight lessons. Let's look ahead to what we'll be studying:

Lesson 1 – Introduction and Overview
Lesson 2 – The Great Disappearing
Lesson 3 – The Role of America in the End Times
Lesson 4 – The Islamic Invasion of Israel
Lesson 5 – The Great Deceiver and His Mark
Lesson 6 – The Birth of a New World Order
Lesson 7 – The Rebuilding of the Temple
Lesson 8 – The Glorious Appearing

Here are three important questions that I am asked everywhere I speak across America and the world:

1. Could we really be in the last days?
2. Is Jesus really going to come again – and could it be today – or tomorrow?
3. What indicators are present that would cause me to believe that time is short?

Be assured that we will address all three questions in detail and give you Bible-based answers.

For many years now, I have made a habit of beginning every day by walking into my study,

opening my Bible, and looking at two words I have written down in my Bible. The words are "Maybe today." I have a deep conviction that Jesus is coming soon, and that realization colors everything in my life. As we ponder these and other questions and begin this study of Bible prophecy, we need to be aware of two primary schools of thought regarding the return of Jesus.

One school of thought is skeptical and mocking. Some people make light of the idea that we are the terminal generation and that Jesus may be coming back soon. The Apostle Peter was aware of these critics and wrote about them in 2 Peter 3:3-4:

> *"There shall come in the last days scoffers, walking after their own lusts, and saying, Where is the promise of his coming? For since the fathers fell asleep, all things continue as they were from the beginning of the creation."*

These people make fun of the idea that Jesus will return. Just as they existed in New Testament times, scoffers and mockers exist today – both inside and outside of the church. I encourage you to be aware that they are out there.

Another school of thought has its own tailored answer for every single question about prophecy. This school has the audacity to declare that they know every detail, every method, and every facet of what God will do, even up to the date when the Rapture will occur. Such people have been with us throughout human history and have been proven wrong time and time again.

We are not going to focus on either of these two positions. We're going to focus on the only reliable source for what our future holds, and we

1

will also focus on who holds the future. We know that our Lord Jesus Christ is in control. Isaiah 46:9-10 will be our theme verse for this study:

"Remember the former things of old: for I am God, and there is none else; I am God, and there is none like me, declaring the end from the beginning, and from ancient times the things that are not yet done, saying, My counsel shall stand, and I will do all my pleasure."

In this study of future events, we're going to be looking at the big picture. Sometimes people delve into biblical prophecy and get hung up on trying to figure out every little detail. We're not going to be lost in the details because we're going to stay with the big picture throughout these eight lessons. Once you get the big picture, you will be able to understand the snap shots given in Scripture as well. If you stay focused in this study, I promise:

- You will have a new sense of urgency in your spiritual life.
- You will have a new passion.
- Your new passion will be to be more like Jesus – a passion for spiritual purity, prayer, and people – that you might lead them to Jesus Christ who holds our future in his hands.

Initial Statements

As we begin this study together, here are some vital truths I'd like you to keep in mind:

- ➤ The Bible is 28% prophetic. That's right: twenty-eight percent of God's Word is prophecy. We cannot be students of the Word and neglect the body of prophetic teaching in the Bible.
- ➤ There are 1,000 prophecies given in the Bible, and half of them have already been fulfilled.
- ➤ There are 109 specific prophecies related to the first coming of Jesus Christ. There are 327 prophecies related to the second coming of Jesus. Because the advent of Christ into our world was mentioned 109 times in Scripture, how significant must his second coming be when three

times as many prophecies herald his return!
- ➤ Adrian Rogers made this statement and I have never forgotten it: "It's not in the Bible because it's true. It's true because it's in the Bible." I say, "I believe the Bible is true because we have historical documents written by eye witnesses – while other eye witnesses were still alive – that speak to the specific fulfillment of Bible prophecy."

One historic proof of prophetic fulfillment is seen in Matthew 24:1-2 in which Jesus predicts that every stone in the temple will be cast down and broken apart, leaving not a single stone left standing on top of another. In A.D. 70, this prophecy was fulfilled when the Roman Titus broke through the walls of Jerusalem and set fire to the temple. His soldiers, while searching for hidden gold and silver in the temple walls, pried apart every stone in the structure. In A.D. 135, the Roman Hadrian entered Jerusalem and plowed the entire top of the temple mount, turning over every stone. The prophecy of Christ was fulfilled in every detail.
- ➤ Prophecy was never given to *scare* us, but to *prepare* us. God wants us to be prepared for what the future holds and to know that he holds the future. There is no need to be fearful when you know the one who holds your future in his hands.

We are living today in what I call the *stage-setting* – the world stage is being set for the ultimate fulfillment of the return of Jesus Christ. World events are screaming in our time that Jesus is coming soon. Here are four reasons I believe we are living in the last days.

1. **It is our generation that has seen the return of the Jews to the Holy Land.** Israel's rebirth is a monumental event in world history.
2. **It is our generation that has experienced the explosion of technology.** We can watch events happen in real time on the other side of the world, and we can see biblical prophecies fulfilled that are setting the stage for Christ's return.

3. **We now have the capability to destroy the world.** Both stable nations and rogue nations possess nuclear weapons; and we live in a world in which the goal of some is death, martyrdom, and the extinction of their enemies. Indeed, we live in perilous times.

4. **We have in the church today unprecedented apostasy (abandonment of faith).** The Internet has made it possible to spread heresy and apostasy easily and instantly to millions of bewildered, innocent seekers.

Truly the world stage is set for prophecy to be fulfilled, and it is important for believers and even non-believers to understand what God's Word is saying to us in these end times. We must understand and be ready! I am excited about journeying with you through these eight lessons and developing an urgency for living and a new passion to be more like Jesus. It is in his hands that our future rests.

DISCUSSION

1. We know that 28% of the Bible is prophetic in nature. Regardless of how much or how little you may know about the end times, are you excited or do you feel a little overwhelmed about digging into biblical prophecy? Explain.

_____

_____

2. On a scale of 1 to 5, how often do you think about the return of Christ?

1	2	3	4	5
Rarely		Occasionally		Frequently

Why is the return of Christ in your thoughts rarely/occasionally/frequently? Discuss your responses.

3. Jesus' disciples asked him why he used stories or parables when speaking to people. Turn to Matthew 13:10-17 and summarize Jesus' answer in the space below.

_____

_____

4. Understanding God's Word is not always easy, but the Holy Spirit gives us "eyes to see and ears to hear." Jesus said that the Kingdom of God remains a mystery to some people. Why do you suppose events surrounding the end days are veiled in mystery?

_____

_____

5. Let's review the four reasons why we could be living in the last days. Which of these reasons is/are most significant in your mind and why? Discuss your thoughts with the group.

Four Reasons	Why is this significant to you?
1. Return of the Jews to the Holy Land	
2. Explosion of technology	
3. Humanity's capacity to destroy the world	
4. Unprecedented apostasy in the church	

3

LIFESCENE

Darryl is an active church member who believes that studying biblical prophecy is a waste of time, and he criticizes his pastor every time he preaches on it. In the past, Darryl was open to considering the subject, but charlatans and TV preachers have left him with a bad taste in his mouth for anything prophetic. Darryl spent thousands of dollars preparing for predicted Y2K disasters that never happened, and this turned him off even more to doomsday scenarios. He now believes that anyone who tries to predict or explain anything about the future is only "in it for the money." He was even somewhat critical of offering this course in your church.

Do you think it is possible to have a meaningful conversation with Darryl on biblical prophecy? If so, what would you say? How would you approach the conversation? Share your ideas with the group.

_____

_____

APPLICATION

6. Remember this promise: If you stay focused and faithful in this study, you will gain a new sense of urgency and a new passion for godly living, prayer and evangelism. Which of the following would you like to experience most in your life as a result of this study? Share with the group.

I would like to experience . . .	Why?
1. A new sense of urgency in my spiritual life	
2. A passion to be more like Jesus	
3. A passion for spiritual maturity	
4. A passion for prayer	
5. A passion for people – to lead them to Christ.	

PRAYER

Father, bless and enlighten me now as I open my heart and mind to the truth of your Word. Give me an urgency to live for you and reach out to others. In Jesus' name, Amen.

NOTES

_____

_____

_____

_____

The Great Disappearing

As I shared in lesson 1, we are living today in what I call the "stage-setting era." The world stage is being set for the ultimate fulfillment of the return of Jesus Christ. World events are screaming that Jesus is coming soon, and the period in which we are living will draw to its end in an event known as the Rapture. When the Rapture occurs – I like to refer to it as the "Great Disappearing" – Christ will receive unto himself every person on this planet who has trusted him as Savior and Lord.

Critics and skeptics point out that because the word "rapture" never appears in Scripture, the whole idea of a divine gathering of the church in the end times is ludicrous. The word "rapture" comes from the Latin word, *rapturo*, which has its root in the Greek word *harpadzo* meaning "to catch up" or "snatch up." Because the New Testament was written in Koine Greek and later translated into Latin, the Latin word *rapturo* came into English as "rapture." Although the English word "rapture" does not appear in the Bible, the statements about this prophetic event are nonetheless true. Jesus himself talked clearly about the gathering of the church in John 14:1-3:

> Let not your heart be troubled: ye believe in God, believe also in me. In my Father's house are many mansions: if it were not so, I would have told you. I go to prepare a place for you. And if I go and prepare a place for you, I will come again, and receive you unto myself; that where I am, there ye may be also.

Sometimes students of Bible prophecy can become confused about the Rapture and the Second Coming of Christ. The key to understanding these two events is in the prepositions. The Rapture or Great Disappearing is the coming of Christ *for* the saints, and the Second Coming of Christ is the coming of Christ *with* the saints. These two events will be separated in time by at least seven years. To contrast the differences between these two events, I have borrowed the following chart from a friend.

Rapture/Blessed Hope	Second Coming/Glorious Appearing
1-Christ comes in the air *for* his own	1-Christ comes *with* his own to earth
2-Rapture/translation of all Christians	2-No one is translated
3-Christians are taken to the Father's house	3-Resurrected saints do not see the Father's house
4-No judgment on earth at the Rapture	4-Christ judges inhabitants of the earth
5-The church is taken to heaven at Rapture	5-Christ sets up his Kingdom on earth
6-The Rapture is imminent	6-Can't occur for at least seven years
7-No signs for Rapture	7-Many signs for Christ's physical coming
8-For believers only	8-Affects all mankind
	9-Time of mourning
9-Time of joy	10-Immediately after Tribulation
10-Comes before the Day of Wrath	11-Satan bound for 1,000 years
11-No mention of Satan	12-No time or place for Judgment Seat
12-The Judgment Seat of Christ	13-His bride descends with him
13-Marriage of the Lamb	14-Every eye shall see him
14-Only his own see him	15-1,000-year Kingdom begins
15-The Tribulation begins	

As we look further in this study at the coming of Christ for the saints, we will organize our thoughts around four key words: *promise, participant, process,* and *plan.* Although there are many verses in the Bible that speak to this event, these following three passages will form the basis for our study of the Rapture: John 14:1-6; 1 Thessalonians 4:16-18; 1 Corinthians 15:51-54.

The Promise

In John 14:1-3, printed above, Jesus clearly promises that he will return to receive his followers. Jesus will bring believers to the place he has prepared for them in his Father's house, which is heaven. He tells his disciples in John 14 that he is soon going to leave them but that he will return. He who went away will one day return. He didn't *hint* at his return: He *promised* it! In 1 Thessalonians 4:14, the Apostle Paul reiterates what New Testament believers knew to be true:

> For if we believe that Jesus died and rose again, even so them also which sleep in Jesus will God bring with him.

The promise of the Great Disappearing should be an encouraging, motivating reality for Christians – a hope that creates an expectancy and an enduring passion for the Lord in the midst of the struggles of this age.

The Participants

Only those who believe in God will participate in this disappearing. In John 14:1, Jesus said to his disciples, "ye believe in God, believe also in me." In Acts 16:31, the Apostle Paul tells the keeper of the prison to "believe on the Lord Jesus Christ, and thou shalt be saved, and thy house." But believing that Jesus Christ is the Son of God is not what defines a Christ-follower – a Christian. James 2:19 states that "the devils also believe, and tremble," yet they are not followers of Christ. A Christian not only believes in the reality of Jesus Christ as the Savior of the world and Son of God, but places his trust in and reliance upon Jesus Christ.

Allow me to illustrate. If you were to watch me successfully walk a tightrope 100 feet above the ground – without a safety net – you would *believe* that I could walk a tightrope. Such belief is easy: you have seen me do it. How would you respond if I invited you to sit on my shoulders while I repeated the feat 100 feet above the ground without a net? Does your belief translate into a trust upon which you will risk your life? A clear sign that a person both *believes* and *trusts* in Christ is that person's obedience to the Word of God. Only those who have moved from intellectual assent to complete trust in Christ as their Savior and Lord will obey his Word and participate in the Rapture. Have you trusted Christ? Are you trusting him now?

The Process

The Great Disappearing will follow a process already outlined in Scripture. God has given us an understanding of the process so we will not fear, but be comforted and reassured that he is sovereign and all powerful. Let's examine the process in 1 Thessalonians 4:16-18:

> For the Lord himself shall descend from heaven with a shout, with the voice of the archangel, and with the trump of God: and the dead in Christ shall rise first: then we which are alive and remain shall be caught up together with them in the clouds, to meet the Lord in the air: and so shall we ever be with the Lord. Wherefore comfort one another with these words.

As the Lord descends from heaven, we will hear the shout of an archangel, and the trumpet of God will herald Christ's arrival. Believers who have already died will be raised to meet Christ in the air. Then all Christians who are alive at that moment will be caught up to meet Christ in the clouds. At that moment all believers – formerly deceased and those still alive – will receive their glorified bodies. From that moment and into eternity, all living and deceased believers will live with Christ in the place he has prepared for us. Knowing God's process can bring believers great comfort, especially in knowing with certainty that saved loved ones who are already with Christ and who already possess bodies suitable for their heavenly existence, will receive glorified, resurrected bodies just like those of us who are alive, as we shall both know and be known.

The Plan

God's plan for this glorious reunion, this Great Disappearing, is part of his great plan of the ages. As Jesus told us in John 14, he has gone ahead to prepare a place for us. The illustration Jesus used in this scripture recalls the first-century Jewish wedding tradition known well among Jesus' contemporaries. When a man and woman became engaged, the husband began immediately to build onto his home, or prepare a place at his parents' home for him and his bride to live. The bride did not set a date for the wedding because she did not know when her new home would be ready. The wedding would occur immediately whenever the new home was complete. Not knowing how long the remodeling or construction would take, the bride quickly prepared herself, made appropriate plans, and remained alert and ready for word that her new home was ready and that the wedding would

occur. The point is: she lived in an attitude of expectancy and readiness.

Jesus told us in Matthew 24:36 and Mark 13:32 that no one knows the day when Christ will come for the saints. Not even he knew! Only God the Father knows when that great day will arrive. God has a plan for the ages that will be sudden and unpredictable in timing, and yet as certain as the dawn of a new day. His plan for believers is that they be prepared and ready, looking forward to Christ's arrival.

Jesus warned us thirteen times in the New Testament to watch for the signs of his return and to be ready. The key word repeated over and over is the word "watch" – be looking for the time when Christ returns for his church. Jesus wanted us to be excited about his return, motivated, and focused so we would feel compelled to share our faith with as many people as possible in the time we have left. Are you focused and busy about the Master's business.

DISCUSSION

1. In the past whenever you have read or thought about the Rapture, have you had questions, fears, or hopes? Jot down your thoughts and share them with the group.

_____

_____

2. Take a moment to re-read the promise in John 14:1-3, the passage concerning "let not your heart be troubled... " How has this scripture comforted and encouraged you at difficult times in your life?

_____

_____

3. Review the section above concerning who will be taking part in the Rapture. To what degree are you confident that you will be included in those who are to be caught up to meet Christ in the air? Why? Write your response in the space below.

0 %	25%	50%	75%	100%
I know I am not included	I doubt whether I will be included	I may or may not be included	I hope I will be included	I am certain I will be included

I am _____ % confident. (If you indicated less than 100%, this study will be a confidence-builder.)

4. Re-read 1 Thessalonians 4:16-18 and recall the sequence of Christ's return for believers (next page).

1. _____   3. _____

2. _____   4. _____

LIFESCENE

Reese has been a Christian for many years now and is active in her church. Like many believers, she has good days and bad days and struggles with issues in her family, her job, and her life. Sometimes the cares of life and the continuing discouragements she faces at home cause her to doubt her salvation and temporarily abandon her church and Christian friends. Sometimes she wonders why being a Christian doesn't solve all the problems she faces. In fact, life often seems harder and more painful when she attempts to obey what she reads in the Bible. She looks at the lives of others in her church and wonders why they show hope and trust when they have lost family members in death or have experienced great losses. Reese confides in you one day that she must be a failure as a Christian and wonders why there isn't more to Christianity than struggle and problems.

What do you say to Reese? Does anything in this lesson relate to her situation? What are your thoughts?

_____

_____

APPLICATON

5. Do you know anyone whom you suspect might not participate in the Rapture if it occurred today? Write the names here, pray for them daily and look for opportunity to share Christ with them.

_____

_____

6. Now that you know the *promise*, the *participants*, the *process*, and the *plan* of the Rapture, what difference does it make? What impact, if any, does the Great Disappearing have on your life and outlook?

_____

_____

PRAYER

Thank you, Lord, for the promise of your return for believers everywhere and for preparing a place for us in heaven. I always want to live a life worthy of your love and favor. In Jesus' name, Amen.

Lesson 3

The Role of America in the End Times

On many occasions I have pondered in my heart where America would be in the last days and how the demise of this great country might possibly come about. When I travel and speak in churches across the country, people often ask me why America is not mentioned in Scripture and what will happen to America in the end times. These are two very interesting questions, and in this lesson we will focus on what may be the role of America in the last days.

Contrary to what the *Book of Mormon* teaches, America is not mentioned in Scripture. The Americas were not known to the human authors of the Old and New Testaments because the canon of Scripture was closed in A.D. 325—more than 1100 years before America was discovered by the civilized world. Unfortunately, some interpreters of Scripture and biblical prophecy have tried to fit the United States into Scripture by taking verses out of context and ignoring historical and cultural information relevant to sound biblical interpretation. Many such attempts have been made to "insert" America into Bible prophecy, but none of them can be supported biblically or contextually.

Why is America not mentioned in the Bible, especially within the context of end time prophecy? In addition to the obvious time factor mentioned above, there are at least two possible reasons, neither of which can be confirmed until Christ returns for the saints.

1. It is possible that America is not mentioned because she will be destroyed by her enemies before the Tribulation begins.
2. It is possible that America is not mentioned because through moral, spiritual, and economic decline, America may implode from

within. I am reminded of the ancient admonition found in Proverbs 14:34: "Righteousness exalteth a nation: but sin is a reproach to any people."

Recently I read George Friedman's book, *The Next 100 Years: A Forecast for the 21st Century*, published in 2009. Friedman states "the United States will be the dominant power in the coming century because of its overwhelming economic and military power." As I read the book, I was reminded that Friedman was viewing the world through a social and economic lens and not a spiritual one. As such, he is totally disconnected from spiritual reality.

In 1 Corinthians 2:14, Paul instructed the church at Corinth that "the natural man receiveth not the things of the Spirit of God: for they are foolishness unto him: neither can he know them, because they are spiritually discerned." As much as I love America and the role we have been given to play in human history, I know that our nation is facing enormous pressures within and without, all of which will play a role in our destiny. As we consider the role that America will play in the end times, we must face four current realities.

Potential Economic Collapse

- The current indebtedness of our nation is pushing 15 trillion dollars. Much of our current debt load is being financed by China.
- Home values continue to drop. As of this writing, approximately 28% of all homeowners in our country owe more on their home loans than those homes are worth. More than one in four homeowners is under water or "upside down" in their mortgage.

- Foreign imports are vastly outstripping American exports.
- According to recent reports, China's economy will surpass the United States economy by 2016, if not before.
- Unemployment continues to rise. When you include the hundreds of thousands of Americans who have given up looking for a job, unemployment in our nation is approximately 16%. Approximately 13% of Americans receive food stamps monthly.
- Nearly half of all Americans do not pay any federal income tax. In fact, only 53% of all eligible tax payers pay any federal income tax.
- In addition to the federal government's deficit spending, 46 states are on the verge of bankruptcy.
- The nations of Russia, China, and Japan are calling for the dollar to be replaced by another monetary instrument as the world reserve currency.

Crippling Terrorist Attack

Even though the United States has rebounded from the terrorist attacks of 9/11, we continue to live under the constant awareness of terrorism and the incredible impact it has on our safety and financial stability. Terrorism has changed the life-style of millions of Americans within only one decade. Hundreds of millions of dollars are channeled into protecting us from acts of terrorism, not to mention the staggering costs in human lives in conflicts in Afghanistan, Iraq, and other areas of the world. The cost of combating terrorism will eventually surpass the cost of the Cold War with the former Soviet Union.

The Rapture

When the Rapture occurs, how many Americans will disappear into the clouds to be with the Lord? According to polling done by George Barna, fewer than half of Americans refer to themselves as "born again." A much smaller percentage claims to be "evangelical." Christians play a vital role in all facets of American life, including charitable organizations, disaster relief, and other organizations that care for the physical and spiritual needs of others. What will happen to America after the Rapture? I shudder to think

about what will become of this great nation when believers have left this earth.

Cultural and Moral Shifts

Many of us today can remember numerous events and trends that have shifted the moral landscape of our nation. What once seemed impossible and unthinkable has become the norm, the "thinking" of our day. During our lifetimes, we have seen the following:

- The once-popular belief in a creator God who created all that exists has been usurped by the theory of evolution. Millions today have bought into Darwin's *Origin of the Species* as fact and ignore the fact that Darwin himself stated it was only a theory.
- In 1962, the U.S. Supreme Court determined that it is unconstitutional for state officials to compose an official school prayer and require its recitation in public schools. The next year the court declared school-sponsored Bible reading in public schools unconstitutional.
- In 1973, the Supreme Court established the legality of abortion by deciding that the right to privacy under the due process clause in the Constitution extends to a woman's decision to have an abortion.
- The successful promotion of the gay rights agenda in the U.S. has led to significant revision in federal, state, and local legislation and public policy and has become part of the curriculum in many public schools.

In the midst of current economic travails, the war on terror, and the reality of a post-rapture America, I have heard some people predict that God will judge America some day. *I believe he is already judging America.* I do not know what happens to America in the last days, but we are on course toward the decline and eventual demise of America. Yes, we are living in perilous times.

The Bible is replete with names of nations and tribes that no longer exist: the Moabites, the Hittites, the Ammonites, the Edomites, and scores of other people groups. All of these and more have passed into the dust bin of history.

Will the day come in the not too distant future when someone might ask, "Did you ever meet an American?"

In Hebrews 11, we find the believers' roll call of faith, a record of biblical saints who through faith understood that this world was not their home. Note particularly in verses 13-16 how they saw their time here on earth.

> These all died in faith, not having received the promises, but having seen them afar off, and were persuaded of them, and embraced them, and confessed that they were strangers and pilgrims on the earth. For they that say such things declare plainly that they seek a country. And truly, if they had been mindful of that country from whence they came out, they might have had opportunity to have returned. But now they desire a better country, that is, an heavenly: wherefore God is not ashamed to be called their God: for he hath prepared for them a city.

Believers know that they are strangers and pilgrims on this earth, and they know that the Lord Jesus Christ is preparing a much, much better place as their eternal home. Everything we love, honor, and value in this great nation pales in comparison to the heavenly city that awaits us when our Lord returns. In Revelation 22:20, our Savior tells us, "Surely I come quickly." And all the saints of God reply, "Amen. Even so, come, Lord Jesus."

DISCUSSION

1. Of all the lessons in this study, this lesson on the role of America in the end times may be the most sobering. Having listened to and viewed this lesson, what are your thoughts and feelings at this point in the study? Write down your thoughts and share them with the group.

   _____

   _____

2. Turn to 1 Peter 2:11-17. Peter's words were originally directed to Jewish believers scattered throughout Pontus, Galatia, Cappadocia, Asia, and Bithynia. Through the inspiration of the Holy Spirit, Peter's words speak to us today. How does this passage of scripture address the attitude and behavior of Christians living in this nation in the 21st century?

   _____

   _____

3. After studying this lesson, your mind is probably full of thoughts and intercessory prayers you want to lift to the Lord. Take a moment and write down words, phrases and concerns you want to pray in light of this lesson. After you have listed your prayer concerns, share them with the group and refer to this page as a prayer guide in the week ahead.

   _____

   _____

LIFESCENE

Tom and Barbara are a married couple who attend an evangelical church in their city. Although they have been married for more than 20 years and see eye-to-eye on many issues, they disagree strongly about the future of America and American life. Tom believes that America has been chosen

by God to bring the Gospel to a dark and lost world and that God's hand of blessing and protection is upon the United States. Tom believes God is the refuge and stronghold for the United States and will save our nation from its enemies. Barbara believes that God has judged America, found America guilty of abandoning him, and is now judging the nation. She feels certain without a doubt that America's days are numbered and soon the nation will fall as did the Roman Empire.

If Tom and Barbara were to sit down and share with you their opposing views of God and America, how would you respond? Jot down your thoughts and share them with the group.

_____

_____

APPLICATION

4. Some Christians may think that because they will not be here after the Rapture, their role in our nation from this point forward is not important. After all, they will not be here to deal with the aftermath. But after participating in this lesson, what impact will this lesson have on how you live your life from this day forward? Are any changes called for? Share your thoughts with the group.

_____

_____

5. Read 1 Peter 3 and make your own list of "Seven Ways to Live in the Last Days," drawing from this single chapter in the New Testament.

"Seven Ways to Live in the Last Days"
1.
2.
3.
4.
5.
6.
7.

PRAYER

Lord Jesus, while I cannot change the course of our great nation *by* myself, I commit that I will be responsible *for* myself. I further commit to lead my family to walk obediently before you and remain faithful to Scripture and to the church. I lift our nation and its leaders to you in prayer, that they will acknowledge you and your plan for mankind in all they do, so America can be saved and get back on track under your headship. In Jesus' name, Amen.

The Islamic Invasion of Israel

Throughout the Bible, God has given us much of his plan for the future, and part of that plan includes an intensifying and escalation of already raging battles in the Middle East. I believe that the conflict in Iraq and Afghanistan and the war on terror are just a prelude for what is to come.

The Rapture will set in motion a series of events that will lead to the seven-year Tribulation. I believe that Christians will not be here to experience the horrors that will come in the wake of the Antichrist, nor will we be here to see the Islamic invasion of Israel that will break out in the Middle East following the Rapture. Ezekiel 38 and 39 show us that there will be a regional war in the Middle East, and I believe it occurs just after the Rapture.

At this point, I want to make a disclaimer regarding Muslims: I do not hate Muslims. I have hundreds of Muslim friends in the Middle East, and they are good and decent people. Many in the Muslim world do not subscribe to the terrorists' ideology of death, conquest, and conversion by the sword. But one fact remains: when the peaceful Muslims among us denounce violence, they are in disagreement with their own scripture, the Quran, and with Muhammad, the founding prophet of Islam. Among Islam's core doctrines is the belief that Islam will dominate the earth and that Islamic law will be imposed on a global scale.

Islamic terrorism in our day is a powerful indicator signaling the nearness of Christ's return for his church and a coming war in the Middle East. Radical Islam is waging war with all non-Muslims on three fronts in our world today: Jihad, biological growth, and economic power.

Jihad

Jihad – or "holy war" – is a compulsory attempt to expand territorial Islamic rule, the goal being to achieve Muslim dominion over the entire globe. Jihad in the sense of territorial expansion has been a central aspect of Islam since its inception. Islamic Jihad stands in direct opposition to Christ's Great Commission to make disciples of all nations.

The primary focus of Jihad's aggression is the extermination of Israel and the West. In recent years, Iran's President Ahmadinejad has openly declared his intentions to wipe Israel from the map. In addition, a state-run website in Iran recently heralded the return of Imam Mahdi, who disappeared in A.D. 941. According to Iran, Mahdi will form an army, overcome his arch villain in Jerusalem, and defeat the enemies of Islam in several apocalyptic battles.

Biological Growth

Islam's second front in their war against civilization is in population growth and suicide. Without detonating a single suicide bomb or launching an attack, Islam is defeating the West by slowly becoming a majority people. The Muslim birthrate is four times that of Christians. By 2025, one third of all babies in Europe will be into Muslim families.

Consider current population statistics for persons under the age of 15 in these countries:
   Spain & Germany: 14%
   United Kingdom: 18%
   United States: 21 %
   Saudi Arabia: 39%
   Pakistan: 42%
   Yemen: 47%

Currently there are more than one billion Muslims in the world, and millions of them are willing to die for their faith. Muslim mothers have babies in hopes that they will grow up to become martyrs for Allah. In sharp contrast are American women who have abortions and hope for better careers and more money. Is it any wonder that Muslim influence in the world continues to grow?

Economic Power

In the current global economy, Arab nations have the power to destroy America economically if they can unify and involve other nations. The primary lever for this power is oil and America's dependence on foreign oil. Iran is working to change the way oil is purchased around the world by steadily lobbying to replace the dollar as the global monetary standard with the Euro or other currencies. As we learned in lesson 3, America's own economic crisis weakens our financial stability in the world market and makes us increasingly vulnerable to the considerable economic clout of Arab nations.

The Islamic Invasion of Israel and Two Other Battles

Before we focus on the Islamic invasion as described in Ezekiel 38 and 39, I want to distinguish it from two other future battles also mentioned in the Bible. The Islamic invasion of Israel will be a regional war, and it is not the battle of Armageddon described in Revelation 16. Neither is it the final battle described in Revelation 20 when Satan will be loosed a final time at the end of the 1,000-year reign of Christ on earth (Rev. 20:7-10). In the last battle, Satan, the beast, and the false prophet are cast into the lake of fire and brimstone.

Turn now to Ezekiel 38 in your Bible and read the entire chapter. What is described in this chapter is an end-times scenario that God imparted to his servant Ezekiel more than 2,500 years ago. As you read this chapter, do not be discouraged if you find it difficult to grasp the meaning of these words. Be encouraged, however, because God wants us to know what his Word says. He gave us his Word for our edification, our comfort, and for us to trust in him. He is the God who knows the end from the beginning.

God has already pre-ordained these things to happen, and participants in this invasion have already been determined. God gave us these words so that a future generation can know what to watch for as events begin to unfold. As you read Ezekiel 38, you will notice names that sound totally foreign to you today: Cush, Put, Tubal, Gog, Togarmah, and others. Fortunately, in Genesis 10, God provides a vital genealogy of ancient names. Take a moment and turn to Genesis 10. Starting with these ancient names, we can trace the descendants through history and find their current identities and locations in the world. Notice in Genesis 10 that seven of the eight names are the descendents of Noah and his three sons.

Who Participates in the Islamic Invasion?

As I have studied the names in Ezekiel 38 and the ancient genealogy in Genesis 10, I have developed a table that helps trace and translate who will be involved in the coming Islamic invasion of Israel in the end times.

ANCIENT NAME	MODERN NATION
Magog	Fmr Soviet republics/S. Russia
Meshech	Part of Turkey
Tubal	Part/Turkey, S. Russia/Iran
Persia	Iran
Ethiopia (Cush)	Sudan
Put	Libya/North Africa
Gomer	Central Turkey/Cappadocia
Beth-Togarmah	Eastern Anatolia/Turkey
Many peoples with you	Other Islamic nations

What Will Be the Result?

The stage is being set even now for these Islamic countries, led by Russia, to attack the nation of Israel. These countries think that it is "their" idea to invade Israel and finally realize their goal of destroying the Jewish homeland. Ezekiel 38 reminds us that God will put hooks in their jaws and bring them out. God will use these nations to bring about his end-times plan for the world.

Six times in these verses God says that he will use this war so that "they may know that I am Lord." The might of Israel will not win the day; the hand of God will bring the victory! In Ezekiel 39 we read that the carnage will be so great that it will take seven months to bury the dead. Of course, the Tribulation will last seven years, so this is further evidence that the invasion of Israel will occur just after the Rapture and at the beginning of the Tribulation. It may also be that the invasion occurs in the interim period between the Rapture and the signing of the peace treaty marking the beginning of the Tribulation.

The increase in wars, deception, and suffering around the world as we near the time of even greater chaos can be depressing, but it does not have to be this way. God the Father and Jesus the Son did not give us these signs to *scare* us or to cause us to live in fear. We are given these prophetic words to *prepare* us so that we are eagerly watching for Christ's return. One day soon Christ will return for his church, take us away, and complete God's perfect plan for the ages.

DISCUSSION

1. In the world today, we hear conflicting information about Muslims and Islam. Since 9/11, what have you learned and experienced related to Muslims?

   _____

   _____

2. Review Ezekiel 38 and write in the space below any questions you have about the conflict described in these verses. Share your questions with the group and discuss how future events may unfold after the rapture of all Christians.

   _____

   _____

3. Sometimes the forces of evil can appear overwhelming and unstoppable in our world. But God always has the final word. Take a moment to read Psalm 37 and jot down a few phrases or words that comfort and reassure us in the midst of troubled times.

   _____

   _____

LIFESCENE

Larry Thompson (true story, but not real name) is a Christian missionary in a predominately Muslim country where he has served for many years. Because of increasing persecution of Christians in some countries, we will not mention the country where Larry is serving. On his recent trip to the United States, Larry reported that more and more Muslims are professing faith in Christ in spite of the tremendous pushback from Muslim family members and friends. On multiple occasions, Larry has talked to Muslims who said Jesus appeared to them in a dream and instructed them to go to a certain place and wait for someone to tell them about Jesus. This report from Larry has been repeated over and over again by missionaries in other Muslim-dominated countries. God's Spirit is at work all over the world drawing Muslims to Christ.

How does this good news impact your attitude and relationship with Muslims in your city or neighborhood? Jot down your thoughts and share them with the group.

_____

APPLICATION

4. Does anything you have learned in this lesson change your attitude about the Middle East or talks of peace in the Middle East? Jot down your thoughts and share them with the group.

_____

_____

5. Knowing that several nations will one day join forces and invade Israel, and knowing that through the overwhelming power of God they will be defeated, what issues are you facing in your life that have heretofore seemed overwhelming? What current challenges do you need to submit to the Holy Spirit for his direction? Make some notes and share as a group.

_____

_____

PRAYER

Thank you, Lord, for giving me a glimpse of your plan for creation after you and the great multitude of Christians have experienced the Rapture. I commit to live my life with greater faith and trust in you and to make a difference for good and for God while I can. In Jesus' name, Amen.

NOTES

_____

_____

_____

_____

_____

_____

_____

_____

_____

_____

The Birth of a New World Order

A final world order or empire was prophesied long ago by Daniel in Daniel chapter 2 as he interpreted Nebuchadnezzar's dream of four world empires that will rule on earth before the reign of Christ in the Millennial Kingdom. Here is an outline for Daniel chapter 2:

- The dream *received*—Daniel 2:1-6
- The dream *revealed*—Daniel 2:7-23
- The dream *interpreted*—Daniel 2:24-35

Daniel tells Nebuchadnezzar, "there is a God in heaven that revealeth secrets, and maketh known to the king Nebuchadnezzar what shall be in the latter days" (v. 28). Then in verses 31-35, Daniel describes the great image in Nebuchadnezzar's dream.

> [31]Thou, O king, sawest, and behold a great image. This great image, whose brightness was excellent, stood before thee; and the form thereof was terrible. [32]This image's head was of fine gold, his breast and his arms of silver, his belly and his thighs of brass, [33]His legs of iron, his feet part of iron and part of clay. [34]Thou sawest till that a stone was cut out without hands, which smote the image upon his feet that were of iron and clay, and brake them to pieces. [35]Then was the iron, the clay, the brass, the silver, and the gold, broken to pieces together, and became like the chaff of the summer threshing floors; and the wind carried them away, that no place was found for them: and the stone that smote the image became a great mountain, and filled the whole earth.

The head of the bright, great image is made of gold, signifying the Babylonian Empire. The breast and arms of silver represent the Medo-Persian Empire. The belly and thighs of brass represent the Grecian Empire. The legs of iron and the feet of iron and clay represent the Roman Empire. The old Roman Empire was never defeated but imploded from within. So the feet of iron and clay, representing a mixed ethnicity, will be a final kingdom that will rule the world as a revived form of the Roman Empire.

This final, revived form of the Roman Empire will institute a global system of government. We gain this understanding from the books of Daniel, Revelation, and 2 Thessalonians, among others. Revelation 13:2-4 shows how the entire world will be astonished by the Antichrist and pledge to him their worship and allegiance. The Antichrist will be the object of the world's worship, and his signs and wonders will lead the world to follow him. Second Thessalonians 2:9 also tells us that the whole world will be deceived into following the Antichrist. In Daniel 7:3, we see how the Antichrist will go about usurping power from every nation, government, and leader on the planet. Verse 23 tells us that he will not accomplish this takeover through brute force, but by a careful and calculated use of diplomacy.

Modern Events Fulfill Biblical Prophecy

Now that we have examined the scriptural background for a future global government, let's turn to current events and see how far the world has come in fulfilling Scripture. The process of globalization began in the middle of the 20th century. Scripture predicting the revival of the Roman Empire was fulfilled when in 1948 the Benelux Conference was held with Belgium, Holland and Luxemburg coming together to form what has evolved into the European Union.

In 1957, the Treaties of Rome were signed which established the European Economic Community or EEC and the European Atomic Energy Council, or EAEC. What began in 1957 grew over time as Denmark, Ireland, the United Kingdom, Greece, Portugal, and Spain were added to the European Community. Today the number of nations allied with the European Union is 27, encompassing more than 540 million people with a gross domestic product larger than that of the United States.

Not only did the EU create a common set of laws for the union, it launched a common currency, the Euro, which has overtaken the dollar as the currency of choice in global markets. Since 1999, the dollar's dominance has been eroded by the euro, which represents a larger size economy. More and more countries are adopting the euro as their national currency, and a UN panel of economists has proposed replacing the current US dollar-based system, which has been the world's primary reserve currency.

The EU exists as a powerful confederacy with the original ten nations holding permanent member status while nations who joined later hold only observer status. All of this fits perfectly with the description of the fourth beast in Daniel. The roadmap for the future political system that will be established under the leadership of the Antichrist has already been laid out by the United Nations when it divided the globe into ten bioregions.

The United Nations has long championed the need for a global system of government. There is a spiritual agenda of sorts at the United Nations that expects and eagerly awaits the appearance of a single man who can unite all nations under one centralized, global government. Paul Henry Spaak, Secretary General of the UN from 1957-61 said, "We do not want another committee, we have too many already. What we want is a man of sufficient stature to hold the allegiance of all people, and to lift us out of the economic morass in which we are sinking. . . Send us such a man, and be he god or the devil, we will receive him."

National Voices in Favor of a New World Order

For many years, various voices in American government have been heralding and promoting the arrival of a new world order, a unified global government whose authority supersedes that of any single nation. Henry Kissinger once said of free trade, "The North American Free Trade Agreement (NAFTA) is a major stepping stone to the New World Order."

David Rockefeller, chairman of the Trilateral Commission and the Council on Foreign Relations, once said, "We are on the verge of a global transformation. All we need is the right major crisis, and the nations will accept the New World Order."

President Jimmy Carter's National Security Advisor Zbigniew Brzezinski said, "This regionalization of the world is in keeping with the Trilateral Plan which calls for a gradual convergence of East and West, ultimately leading toward the goal of a one-world government. National sovereignty is no longer a viable concept."

In March of 1993, Bill Clinton told USA Today, "We can't be so fixated on our desire to preserve the rights of ordinary Americans." When America's economy is devastated by the disappearance of millions of Americans in the rapture, the United States will return to her roots and look to Europe for leadership. The European Union awaits only the right man to lead the world down a path to destruction.

Some may ask, "How is it possible for a one-world government to exist in a world as fractured and conflicted as our world today?" As fragmented as our world may be, several key developments in our generation have come together to make a one-world government not only possible but highly probable. Consider these seven elements that must be present for a one-world government. Check each element that you believe already exists in our time.

- Ability to communicate in real time
- Accessibility to common markets
- Adoption of a universal language
- Availability of rapid transportation
- Acknowledgement of the absolute necessity for global security
- Acceptance of a common currency that will lead to a cashless society

- Abandonment of national sovereignty and individual rights for the greater good of mankind

The ability to enforce the worship of the Antichrist on a global scale and to regulate who may buy or sell around the world could only be accomplished in a global system of government and through tight control of the world's economy. This global super-state is being created now, in our time, through the continuing empowerment of the European Union and the efforts of the United Nations. The final world government will be a diverse group of nations – a mixture of iron and clay just like in Nebuchadnezzar's dream – under the leadership of the Antichrist and his False Prophet. Europe is paving the way toward a technology-driven world that gives regional governments greater control over every person on the planet.

DISCUSSION

1. When you consider biblical prophecy of a coming one-world government, do you believe that such a government is in the near future or still many years away? Share your opinion and discuss with the group why you hold this position.

_____

_____

2. In addition to the indicators mentioned in this lesson, do you see additional signs that seem to point toward a new world order or a global, unified government? Talk about it as a group.

_____

_____

3. Take a moment to read these two scripture passages that relate to a believer's relationship to government: Matthew 22:15-22 and Romans 13:1-7. What do you think the Christian's role is in a world in which national autonomy is being eroded in favor of a one-world government? Make some notes below and discuss together.

_____

_____

LIFESCENE

Constance has been known to think differently from many of her friends. She proudly sports a "Coexist" bumper sticker on her car, participates in protests for liberal political causes, and often refers to the United States as "the great Satan." She is unswerving in her belief that the U.S. is responsible for most of the ills in the world. She believes that American hubris, big oil, and bigoted patriotism have created unjust wars in Iraq and Afghanistan. She speaks out against what she sees as American imperialism and intolerance of Muslims, lesbians and gays, and minorities. Constance believes that America needs to become a better citizen in the world, stop its egotistic "cowboy diplomacy," and follow the example of more advanced, more tolerant socialistic governments in Europe. She sees herself as a citizen of the world and is embarrassed by the American government. One day you and Constance are having coffee together, and the subject gets around to "what the world is going to be like in the future."

Based on your understanding of biblical prophecy, the new world order, and the coming Antichrist, in what ways will your opinions differ from those of Constance? Will any of your points of view be similar? Jot down your thoughts and discuss your ideas with the group.

_____

_____

APPLICATION

4. Knowing that Christians will be taken from the scene at the Rapture, does the gradual but unstoppable shift to a new world order change the way you think about the United States? The world? Does your knowledge and awareness of a shift to a one-world government call for any change in the way you live today? Discuss your thoughts and make some notes.

_____

_____

5. Read 2 Corinthians 5:14-21. How are we to live out our role as Christ's ambassadors in a world that is moving rapidly toward the end times? Take a few moments to discuss this.

_____

_____

PRAYER

Thank you, Lord, for opening my eyes to your divine plan – a plan not just for my life, but for the entire world you have created. I ask for greater awareness and sensitivity to what you are doing to fulfill the prophecy your Word teaches. Open my eyes to the urgency of these days so I may seize every opportunity to stand tall in the Christian faith and proudly acknowledge that I am yours and you are mine. I want to be a tool in your hands to set a worthy example as a believer and lead others to a personal faith in you. With a humble and grateful heart, I make this prayer in Jesus' name, Amen.

NOTES

_____

_____

_____

_____

Lesson 6

The Great Deceiver and His Mark

The Bible clearly teaches that the Antichrist will be a key figure in the end times. Some people wonder if such a person really exists or if he is a myth. If there is such a character, who or what is he and when will we know he has made his appearance in the world? Regardless of the many questions surrounding the dreaded personification of evil, the arrival of the Antichrist on the world scene will mark the birth of a new world order.

Before we begin this study of the Antichrist, I want to reiterate **that *those of us who have put our faith in Jesus Christ prior to the Rapture of the church will not be here for any of the events discussed in this lesson.*** True believers will not see the invasion of Israel, and we will never know who the Antichrist is because he will arrive on the scene after we have been translated into heaven in the Rapture. I do believe, however, this final imposter is alive today and is waiting in the wings for the right time to step onto the world stage. He will offer his answer to a desperate people in a time of utter chaos and confusion.

To understand who the Antichrist is, we first need to look again at Daniel chapter two and chapter seven. In Daniel 7, Daniel's dream of four beasts represents four world empires that would rule on the earth from Daniel's time until Christ's return. These four world empires have been Babylon, the Medo-Persian Empire, the Grecian Empire, and the Roman Empire. All of these empires rose and fell. In Daniel 2, we see these same four future world empires described in the interpretations of Nebuchadnezzar's dream of a great statue. These two dreams in the Book of Daniel give us a composite picture of what the world political system will look like when the Antichrist rules for seven years.

Daniel's dream of four beasts is also important because it is telling us what is going to happen in the end times, after the Rapture. When the Antichrist is unveiled, he will subdue three of the ten Kings. Indwelt by Satan, he will deceive the world with the "great lie" that he is God, sign a peace treaty with Israel, and begin what will be a seven-year tyrannical rule over the earth – the Great Tribulation.

The Antichrist's Ability to Deceive

John's revelation gives us insight into the Antichrist's motives for establishing his global empire. Revelation 13 says that the Antichrist will speak like a dragon but will have horns like a lamb. In other words, he will speak like Satan but will appear to be Jesus and the fulfillment of Christ's return. He will be an imposter and will do everything he can, including miracles, signs, and wonders, to convince the world that he fulfills all of the messianic prophecies in the Bible.

Revelation 13:3 tells us that the Antichrist will seem to have received a fatal wound. Following this seemingly fatal wound, he will be miraculously healed, astonishing the world and convincing man that he is worthy of their trust and worship. People around the world will see this miraculous healing and resurrection and sell their souls to the devil to follow him.

Scripture provides five specific facts that help identify the Antichrist.

1. He will rise to power out of the revived form of the old Roman Empire, which is now in existence as the European Union.

2. He will come to power sometime after the Rapture of the church and will enter into

a seven-year covenant with Israel that will lead to rebuilding the Temple and resuming the Jewish sacrificial system.

3. Daniel 8:24-25 tells us that he will come to power through deception. He will be a master of intrigue and elevate himself above God by offering peace and security to a war-torn world. All of his diplomatic efforts will succeed, and every nation will consent to the Antichrist's global ambitions. Daniel 7:20 says that he will be an intelligent man with unique powers of persuasion. In other words, he will be the consummate politician.

4. The rise to power of the Antichrist will occur after the Rapture of the church. He will not reveal himself or his deceptive plan until after the departure of the church. In 2 Thessalonians, Paul says that while the power of lawlessness is already at work, the Lawless one, or Antichrist, will not be revealed until the one who restrains is taken out of the way. It is the presence of the Holy Spirit in the hearts of every believer that prevents Satan's evil scheme from being carried out now.

5. The global, political, and economic system used by the Antichrist will be made possible by the use of technology. Those who once rejected technology as a threat to privacy and personal freedoms will submit to the authority of the Antichrist in the name of security.

The Mark of the Beast

Revelation 13, 17, and 18 describe what a world under the Antichrist's rule will look like during the Great Tribulation. During this time, the Antichrist and the False Prophet will have total control of the world's economy, and all commerce on a global scale, as well as at the local level. The False Prophet will be able to exercise this control under the Antichrist's authority by using what Scripture calls the Mark of the Beast.

The purpose of the mark is not necessarily to regulate who may buy and sell, although that's part of it. The main purpose is to force people to worship the Antichrist and to punish those who do not. In Revelation 13:16-17, we learn that the mark will be given on the right hand or on the forehead of those who choose to receive it. A visible mark will be engraved into the flesh of each of the Antichrist's devotees in the form of a tattoo. The mark will incorporate the name of the Beast or the number of his name. The Antichrist and False Prophet will likely incorporate some form of technology into the administration of the mark to track and identify those who are or are not loyal to the Antichrist.

For centuries the idea that one man could control the world's economy and restrict commerce on a global, national, and local level seemed like the stuff of science fiction. But today's rapid technological advances and the rise of the computer age has changed that. The technology for implementing just such a system of marking people and regulating their ability to buy or sell already exists and is in use in many forms around the world. The first decade of the 21st century has seen a steady march toward the global, technology-driven, government-controlled and regulated economy that will allow one man to control everything.

National Identification cards with "smart card" technology will play a large part in a future global system. The Real ID Act of 2005 was passed by the U.S. House of Representatives and later passed by the Senate in 2007. That act, signed into law by President Bush, gives the Secretary of Homeland Security great leeway in regulating a new national I.D. card for every American. Subsection 2 of the Act says, "The secretary shall determine whether a state is meeting the requirements of this section...." There is no specific requirement for a person's ethnicity, religion, or political affiliation to be on the card, but many people are concerned with a requirement found in Title 11, Section 201, Subsection 9, that suggests the use of "a common machine-readable technology, with defined minimum data elements." To reiterate: the Secretary of Homeland Security will have full control over what that identifying information might be.

With national disasters increasing every year, terrorist attacks threatening peace around the globe, and the European Union gaining power globally through regional integration, it is only a matter of time before the rest of the world throws caution to the wind and joins the globalization of a new world order. With each region of the world following the lead of the European Union, the Antichrist will have but to globalize what has already been achieved on a regional basis. The False Prophet will be able to use existing and future technology to monitor every transaction and every person on the planet. Thus shall the personification of evil gain global control for seven dreadful years through the power of deception and technology.

DISCUSSION

1. After completing five of the lessons in this series, we have now focused on the Antichrist and the mark of the beast. Is all of this prophecy coming together for you and becoming clearer, or do you think this is merely just so much science fiction? What are your thoughts at this point? Jot them down and share with the group.

_____

_____

2. Because the Antichrist will rise to deceive and lead after the church has been raptured, what do you believe Christians should do with information now available to them about the rise of the Antichrist and the coming new world order? Note your ideas and share them with the group.

_____

_____

3. Read Daniel 2:44-45. What comfort and reassurance do you gain from the knowledge that the God of heaven will establish – has already established through Christ – a Kingdom that will never be destroyed? Jot down your response and share together.

_____

_____

LIFESCENE

Your neighbor Doug has been leery of government intrusion into his life for years. Recent events since 9/11 and the impact of anti-terrorism policies at airports and other public places have convinced Doug that the Antichrist is already in charge of every facet of American life. Some days Doug believes that the Antichrist is the President of the United States; other days, the secretary general of the United Nations or the head of the IRS. Doug is becoming increasingly skeptical of government and is antagonistic toward any government agency that seems to be spying on him or restricting his freedom as a U.S. citizen. Doug has begun fortifying his home with armaments, supplies, and other necessities to survive what he believes will be an imminent invasion by the new world order. Through over-the-fence conversations in your backyard, Doug learns that you have been studying the end times and the Antichrist.

What would you share with Doug about what you have learned in this lesson that might help him re-think his current ideas about the Antichrist and one-world government? Make some notes and discuss your thoughts together.

_____

APPLICATION

4. Consider for a moment the role that technology is playing in your life today. Does the future misuse or abuse of technology in establishing a new world order under the Antichrist influence your current level of comfort or reliance on technology? Should all aspects of technological advancement be eagerly received and incorporated into your life? What is the thinking of the group on this?

_____

_____

5. Has your understanding of the rise of the Antichrist and the coming new world order increased your desire to talk to your family, friends, and neighbors about their need of salvation? Why or why not?

_____

_____

PRAYER

Thank you, Lord, for giving me greater insight into future events that will take place after Christ has come for his church in the Great Disappearing. Now I ask that your Holy Spirit give me a deeper burden and urgency for sharing the Gospel with others while there is still time. In Jesus' name, Amen.

NOTES

_____
_____
_____
_____
_____
_____
_____
_____
_____
_____
_____
_____

The Rebuilding of the Temple

The first Temple built in Jerusalem by Solomon was destroyed by the Babylonians in 586 B.C., 364 years after it was built. The Jews rebuilt the Temple upon returning from Babylonian captivity, and that Temple was enhanced and enlarged during New Testament days. Then on September 8, A.D. 70, the Roman 10th legion led by General Titus sacked Jerusalem, destroyed the Temple, and took with them many of the sacred vessels and religious artifacts from within. This was one of the darkest days in Jewish history as more than one million Jews lost their lives, and the symbol of God's presence among the Jews was no more.

Rebuilding the Temple has been a passionate goal of the Jews for centuries. When Israel became a nation again in 1948, their dream of rebuilding the Temple seemed within their grasp. Rooted in Judaism is the belief that rebuilding the Temple will lead to the coming of the Messiah who will inhabit it and reign over the earth. One Jewish group in particular has been leading an effort to prepare for rebuilding the Temple. The Temple Mount Faithful and the Temple Institute are led by Rabbi Chaim Richmond and Gershon Salomon. Not only do these organizations aim to rebuild the Temple, they also hope to reinstitute the sacrificial system of the Old Testament. In preparation for the day when the Temple will be rebuilt, Richmond and Salomon have been recreating the ancient temple vessels necessary for proper worship in the Temple. They also have been training rabbis for worship ceremonies in accordance with Old Testament laws.

A formidable obstacle stands in their way. The Muslim world believes the fable that it was from Mount Moriah that Mohammed ascended into the sky on his winged steed, El Baruck. From this belief came the Dome of the Rock project in A.D. 687 that led to the massive shrine completed four years later over the rock where Mohammed supposedly took flight to Mecca. The Dome of the Rock is considered by Muslims today to be one of the three holiest areas in Islam. *Rebuilding a Jewish temple on this site will be another of the future events that will shake the world.*

What the Bible Says

There is a group of Christians called amillennialists who believe that the prophecies concerning rebuilding the Temple have been fulfilled already. Although historical events seem to fulfill some of the scriptures that foretell the defiling of the Temple and its utter destruction, one passage of scripture from Daniel 9:26-27 indicates that a future Temple will exist during the Tribulation and reign of the Antichrist.

> *26And after threescore and two weeks shall Messiah be cut off, but not for himself: and the people of the prince that shall come shall destroy the city and the sanctuary; and the end thereof shall be with a flood, and unto the end of the war desolations are determined. 27And he shall confirm the covenant with many for one week: and in the midst of the week he shall cause the sacrifice and the oblation to cease, and for the overspreading of abominations he shall make it desolate, even until the consummation, and that determined shall be poured upon the desolate.*

Daniel tells us that the Antichrist will make a covenant with the many (the Jews) and in the middle of the seven- year Tribulation he will put an end to temple sacrifice and set up the abomination that causes desolation. The abomination is a **reference to the image of the Beast that** the False Prophet will erect on a wing of the Temple during the second half of the Tribulation (Rev. 13:15-15). We know that the Antichrist will come from Rome during the end times, so we can read into it that the Romans were prophesied to destroy the Temple after Christ was cut off. History fulfilled the prophecy.

For the Antichrist to stop temple sacrifice and offerings and defile the Temple with his image, we can conclude from Daniel 9:26-27 that a third Temple will be built and the Jewish sacrificial system reestablished. Daniel 12:11 supports this view.

> [11]And from the time that the daily sacrifice shall be taken away, and the abomination that maketh desolate set up, there shall be a thousand two hundred and ninety days.

This indicates that temple sacrifice will be stopped half way through the Tribulation and three and a half years before Christ returns to defeat the Antichrist and establish his millennial kingdom.

How the Temple Might Be Rebuilt

You may be wondering how the Temple will be rebuilt on the spot where the Dome of the Rock currently stands. As we have learned, the Rapture will be followed by an invasion of Israel that will leave the attacking Islamic nations completely decimated. It is possible that the Dome of the Rock may be taken out of the picture as a result of the war and natural disasters God will use to supernaturally protect Israel from her attackers.

One of the most important peacemaking endeavors that will be undertaken by the Antichrist at the beginning of the Tribulation period will be to finally restore peace to the

Tisha B'Av is an annual fast day in Judaism, named for the ninth day of the month of Av in the Hebrew calendar. Observed in July or August, the fast commemorates the destruction of both the First Temple and Second Temple in Jerusalem, which occurred about 656 years apart, but on the same Hebrew calendar date. The day is called the "saddest day in Jewish history".

The fast lasts about 25 hours, beginning at sunset on the eve of Tisha B'Av and ending at nightfall the next day. In addition to the prohibitions against eating or drinking, observant Jews also observe prohibitions against washing or bathing, applying creams or oils, wearing leather shoes, or having marital relations. In addition, mourning customs similar to those applicable to the shiva period immediately following the death of a close relative are traditionally followed for at least part of the day, including sitting on low stools, refraining from work, and not greeting others.

The Book of Lamentations is traditionally read, followed by the kinnot, a series of liturgical lamentations. In Sephardic communities, it is also customary to read the Book of Job.

~ Excerpted from
http://en.wikipedia.org/wiki/Tisha_B'Av

Middle East. He will do what once seemed impossible and negotiate a peace treaty between Israel, the Palestinians, and the Arab world. His success as a negotiator may be possible if the Arab world sees the Antichrist as the returning 12th Imam of Islamic prophecy. Islamic leaders are already preparing for the Imam's return and have indicated that they believe the Mahdi's return is only a few years away. With the Arab world having suffered a devastating loss following their invasion of Israel, the Mahdi's return might represent at least a spiritual victory for the Islamic faith. How tempting it will be for a defeated people to place their hope in a man who may have arrived on the scene to snatch victory from the jaws of defeat and restore their honor. The Antichrist will be able to convince the warring sides in the Middle East to put aside their differences and begin the rebuilding of the

Temple. A long sought-after peace will seem to overtake the planet almost overnight. This peace, however, will be a false peace, an illusion designed to hide the Antichrist's true plans.

The first three and a half years of the Tribulation will be relatively peaceful under the Antichrist's reign and will give the remaining inhabitants of the earth a false sense of hope and security. The Antichrist will seize upon people's desperate need to rebuild something better from the rubble left behind, and his mastery of diplomacy will be put to speedy use around the world. But three and a half years after the Tribulation begins, the peace negotiated by the Antichrist will disintegrate and the second half of the Tribulation will begin the "Great" Tribulation.

The Great Tribulation will be a time of punishment and wrath on earth that will begin when the Antichrist breaks the covenant he made with Israel and brings an end to the Jewish system of sacrifice. Even more insulting to the Jewish people will be the image of the Antichrist erected by the false prophet, his partner in sin, on a wing of the rebuilt Temple. The Antichrist will declare to the world that he is the god of the universe. Having suffered a seemingly fatal wound and supposedly come back to life, he will claim to be the returned Christ, the Imam Mahdi, and the fulfillment of every religion on earth. Every person will be required under penalty of death to worship the Antichrist and bow before the image of the beast before receiving their mark of loyalty.

Yes, where the Dome of the Rock now dominates the Jerusalem skyline, a Jewish Temple will one day be rebuilt in all its glory. The nation of Israel will rejoice as the Old Testament sacrificial system is reestablished. But the rejoicing and celebration of Israel will last only for a short time as the Antichrist reveals his true nature and the world enters the darkest period of its history.

DISCUSSION

1. For generations, American presidents and other world leaders have attempted to negotiate peace between Israel, the Palestinians, and Israel's Arab neighbors. Why do you think all of these attempts have been unsuccessful? Jot down your thoughts and share them with the group.

_____

_____

2. Review the information in the sidebar above on the Jewish day of fasting known as Tisha B'Av. Why do you think orthodox Jews continue to observe this day of fasting nearly 2,000 years after the destruction of the last Temple? Write down your thoughts and discuss them together.

_____

_____

3. Read Daniel 11:31 and 2 Thessalonians 2:4. How do these two scripture passages reinforce what you have learned in this lesson?

_____

_____

4. The Temple Mount Faithful and the Temple Institute led by Rabbi Chaim Richmond and Gershon Salomon are preparing for the rebuilding of the Temple and the reestablishment of the Old Testament sacrificial system. When you reflect on the life, sacrificial death, and resurrection of Jesus – the Lamb of God – what are your thoughts and emotions about rebuilding the Temple? Share together.

LIFESCENE

The website for Temple Mount Faithful makes this appeal to anyone interested in supporting the rebuilding of the Jewish temple in Jerusalem: "Your spiritual, moral and financial help is needed now more than at any time in the past. We have now reached a critical stage in our campaign. We are going to undertake very important activities which are needed for this complicated stage. We are soon to see the fulfillment of our vision, but this final stage needs additional efforts. You can give us the means and instruments to carry out these activities. Your financial support is critical to fulfill our holy activities. In this you will be an important part in this godly campaign. All donations will be very much appreciated by G-d and your messengers – the Temple Mount Faithful members. Thank you so much and may the G-d of Israel bless you."

Based on what you have learned in this lesson, do you believe that Christians should or should not provide financial support to the Temple Mount Faithful movement? Jot down your thoughts and share your reasons with the group.

_____

_____

APPLICATION

5. The events described in this lesson will take place after Christians have been taken up into the air to meet the Lord. Based on what you have learned about the events leading up to, surrounding, and following the rebuilding of the Temple, what impact will this information have on your relationship with Christ? Your relationship with unbelievers? With people you know who are Jewish? Write down your thoughts and share together.

_____

_____

PRAYER

Dear Father, give me a burden for all people without Christ, whether they are Jewish or not. I ask you to open doors for me to share my personal testimony with them, about how I became a Christian and how you have changed my life. I make this prayer in Jesus' name, Amen.

NOTES

_____

_____

_____

The Glorious Appearing

During the seven years of tribulation on earth, two great events will take place in heaven: 1) Christ's evaluation and judgment of all believers of all ages as to their works and (2) the Marriage Supper of the Lamb.

The time of evaluation and judgment is described in Ecclesiastes 12:11; 2 Corinthians 5:9-10; Ephesians 5:2-7; and Revelation 19:8. This judgment will be a time of purification of the bride of Christ, the church. Each of us will stand before Christ to be evaluated and judged for the works we have done. Our sins will have been forgiven once and for all by the sacrifice Christ made on the cross, but our actions, thoughts, and the motives for our service will be brought into the light for Christ to evaluate them. We will be rewarded for what we did for Jesus and the proliferation of the Gospel in the short time we have here on earth.

Once again, we must remember that our sin was judged on the cross, where Jesus truly "paid it all." Therefore, we will never stand in judgment as to our salvation. For the believer, the Judgment Seat of Christ is a time when our works following salvation will be evaluated and our rewards will be graciously bestowed on us. Many Christians today are confused concerning this very important issue, feeling that one day every sin they've ever committed will be dragged out and revisited before them. If this were true, then our sins – past, present and future – would not have been covered and washed away by the blood of Christ. Let us remember Psalm 103: 11-12 that says, *For as the heaven is high above the earth, so great is his mercy toward them that fear him. As far as the east is from the west, so far hath he removed our transgressions from us.* Christ has saved us and cleansed us! Never forget this central truth. Rejoice in it daily!

As the seven-year Tribulation is drawing to a close, believers of all ages will participate in the Marriage Supper of the Lamb. Revelation 19:7-9a describes this celebratory event.

> *[7]Let us be glad and rejoice, and give honour to him: for the marriage of the Lamb is come, and his wife hath made herself ready. [8]And to her was granted that she should be arrayed in fine linen, clean and white: for the fine linen is the righteousness of saints. [9]And he saith unto me, Write, Blessed are they which are called unto the marriage supper of the Lamb.*

Jesus Christ the Groom will welcome us to the Supper. As His bridegroom, all of the church of Jesus Christ will be invited. But the Supper will also include distinguished guests: all of the Old Testament and New Testament saints who lived and died before Christ's sacrifice on the cross. This glorious Supper with our Savior will take place right before his Glorious Appearing.

The Glorious Appearing

The return of Christ with the saints is heralded in several books of the Bible.

- Zechariah 14:1-4 – *"Behold, the day of the LORD cometh..."*
- Matthew 24:29-30 – *"they shall see the Son of man coming in the clouds of heaven with power and great glory..."*
- Titus 2:13 – *"Looking for that blessed hope, and the glorious appearing of the great God and our Saviour Jesus Christ..."*
- Rev. 19:11-16 – *"And I saw heaven opened, and behold a white horse; and he that sat upon him was called Faithful and True..."*

The Glorious Appearing of the Lord will be different from the Rapture when Christ returned for his church. At the Glorious Appearing, everyone on earth will see him. Those who survive the Tribulation will take part in the judgment of the nations as recorded in Matthew 25. Those who have received Christ will be placed on his right, and those who have rejected him and followed the Antichrist will be placed on his left. The lost are then sent to hell while the saved enter the Millennial Kingdom with Christ.

Based on Scripture, we know several things about the Glorious Appearing of Christ with the saints.

We know *when* it is going to take place. Daniel 9:27 tells us that the Glorious Appearing will take place seven biblical years after the signing of the peace treaty which marks the beginning of the Tribulation.

We know *where* it is going to take place. Isaiah 63:1-4; Acts 1:10; and Revelation 16:16 confirm that Jesus is coming back to the land of Israel.

We know *who* is going to participate.— Representatives of all those on earth (Rev. 19:17-21) and returning saints will be participants. It is sobering to note that half the people on the earth during the Tribulation will die during this seven-year period.

We know *why* all of this is going to happen. Jesus is coming to take back what rightly belongs to him. He alone is worthy of all praise and worship.

We know *what* the outcome is going to be. The Glorious Appearing will lead to the Battle of Armageddon, which is actually several battles, all of which occur on the day Christ returns. The Antichrist, indwelt by Satan, will rally his forces to make one last attempt to destroy God's city. Satan will be defeated and his armies destroyed in a massive slaughter (Rev. 14). Revelation 19:20 tells us that the Antichrist and the false prophet will be thrown into a fiery lake of burning sulfur. Satan will not be thrown into the fiery lake but will be bound for one thousand years during which Christ will reign over the Millennial Kingdom on earth.

Following the battles, Jesus will judge everyone on earth (Matt. 25:31-46). Believers who were martyred for their faith by the Antichrist will be raised to life and will stand below the altar at Jesus' feet. All other believers will stand at the right hand of Christ. All who have rejected Christ and who either lived or died through the Tribulation without being saved – the goats – will stand on the left side of Christ. At this judgment, billions of people will be standing before the Son of God. Keep in mind, however, that the final sentencing for unbelievers will not take place until the end of the millennium at the Great White Throne Judgment.

After Christ judges the multitudes of people gathered before him, the Millennial Kingdom will begin as Jesus redesigns and restores the earth and creates a new heaven and a new earth. He will refashion the earth into a paradise (Isa. 65:17; 2 Pet. 3:1-16). Those who have died and received glorified bodies will reign with Christ over this new earth for a millennium. This new earth will be populated by believers from throughout the ages, including those who were raptured in their earthly bodies at the glorious appearing.

While Satan is bound during these one thousand years, the only temptations encountered in this new paradise are those of the flesh. Those who came to faith during the Tribulation and survived with earthly bodies will populate the world with a burgeoning new generation of people. People born during the millennium will use their free will to make a choice for Christ or against Christ. There will be no death from sickness or other tragedies, and people will live long lives.

At the end of the Millennial Kingdom will come the Great White Throne Judgment (Rev. 20:5-12). Those who died without accepting Christ will receive their final sentencing and punishment, including those who had not accepted Christ when He returned at the Glorious Appearing. All of these will be thrown into the lake of fire for eternity. By this point in time, God's judgment will have been applied to every single person who has ever lived. When this judgment is complete, Jesus will turn over the Kingdom to God the Father.

The New Jerusalem

God will refashion the earth and heavens one final time and replace them with a new heaven and new earth (Rev. 21:1). Within this new earth will be the Holy City, the New Jerusalem, where all believers will live. This New Jerusalem is the place that Jesus has been preparing for us (John 14:1-3). This new earth will be similar to the Garden of Eden, for in it God will fellowship with all believers much like he did with Adam and Eve. It will truly be "heaven on earth" with no oceans or seas, only one landmass with a huge river that provides an abundance of water. There will be no despair, grief, sadness, pain, guilt, temptation, or any other feeling that we suffered in a previous world where Satan influenced us.

If you are a believer, draw on the tremendous hope you have in the eternity that awaits us and do everything possible to bring as many people with you into the Kingdom of God as you can.

Live your life in such a way that those around you will want to know the reason for the hope that is in you. Then search out those who may want to know Christ.

Let me remind us that God did not give his prophetic Word to merely satisfy our curiosity, but to motivate us with a sense of urgency to godly living, prayer, evangelistic outreach and missions! When we begin to get the truth of his coming deep down in our souls, four things will happen. We will have . . .

- a new passion for Jesus Christ
- a new passion for purity
- a new passion for prayer
- a new passion for people

He which testifieth these things saith, Surely I come quickly. Amen. Even so, come, Lord Jesus (Rev. 22:20).

DISCUSSION

1. As you contemplate the Glorious Appearing of our Lord Jesus Christ, the establishment of his thousand year reign, and the New Jerusalem in which God will fellowship with his children much like he did with Adam and Eve, how does your understanding of these future events color or affect how you see life today? Write down your thoughts and share them with the group.

_____

_____

2. In this lesson, we see Jesus Christ as Judge, Warrior, and Conqueror. Can you reconcile these images of the Christ we will see in the future with your mental image of the Christ of the Gospels? How does the "Christ of the future" change your understanding of him today? Jot down your thoughts.

_____

_____

LIFESCENE

Cal has been attending church for years, but mainly because his wife makes life miserable if he doesn't! He may sleep through a sermon every now and then, but occasionally he listens and is somewhat inspired by the pastor's stories and what he hears about the Bible. Cal does not think of himself as a bad person; in fact, he thinks he is actually a better person than most church members. Over the years he has resisted all efforts to commit his life to Christ, and he tells his wife that he does not want to be a hypocrite like every other person at church. Cal believes that one day, later in life, he will "get right with God" and become a Christian before he dies. But right now, he believes he's better off not pretending to be something he's not. Jesus, repentance, baptism, tithing and all of that religious stuff is just going to have to wait a while.

What have you learned in this study that you could share with Cal to encourage him? What have you learned that would help you challenge the philosophy by which he is living his life? In other words, how can you help a person like Cal? Discuss together.

_____

_____

APPLICATION

3. Has this study on biblical prophecy and the end times given you a new PASSION . . .

    • . . . for **Jesus Christ**? If so, in what way?

    _____

    • . . . for **purity**? If so, in what way?

    _____

    • . . . for **prayer**? If so, in what way?

    _____

    • . . . for **people who do not know Christ**? If so, in what way?

    _____

    Discuss your responses. If time remains, take a few moments to review some high points of the study.

Now that you have completed *It Could Happen Tomorrow,* hopefully you understand more about future events and are more assured than ever as to who holds the future. If you are a follower of Christ, you have the glorious hope of his return at the Great Disappearing, the Millennial Rule of Christ, and the coming of the New Jerusalem when God will dwell with his children in a new heaven and a new earth. My prayer for you is that your gratitude and renewed hope will be reflected in your passion for sharing the Gospel with others while there is still time. After all, Jesus could come tomorrow – or today. GF

PRAYER

Thank you, Lord, for giving me this biblical glimpse into your divine plan for the ages. Help me to become more passionate about living for you, serving you and reaching others. Whether you come today, tomorrow, or years from now, I want to be faithful every day that I live. In Jesus' name, Amen.